The Nature of Canadian Federalism

THE NATURE OF CANADIAN FEDERALISM

BY

W. P. M. KENNEDY, M.A., Litt. D.,
(TRINITY COLLEGE, DUBLIN)

Assistant Professor of History, in the University of Toronto

UNIVERSITY OF TORONTO PRESS.

1921

PREFATORY NOTE.

The Canadian constitution is one of the most interesting and successful of modern experiments in government Its nature and essence are therefore of importance to students of politics, especially at a moment when devolution and federalism are living issues in the British Isles and in the international world.

In the following pages I have attempted to discover the underlying principles of the Canadian constitution, and to illustrate them from constitutional law in such a way as to bring out the established relationship between the central and provincial governments Such relationship is perhaps the most fascinating aspect of non-unitary systems, for it will provide new illustrations of the conception of the state and it will suggest vital questions in connection with the nature of sovereignty

I wish to thank *The Canadian Historical Review* for permission to make use of matter which substantially appeared in its pages My thanks are also due to W Stewart Wallace, Esq , M.A., for giving me the benefit of his expert knowledge of Canadian History; to R M. MacIver, Esq., M A., Phil D , for his kindness in discussing the subject with me and for reading my manuscript, and to the Honourable Mr Justice C. A. Masten for directing me in difficult constitutional questions and for guiding me to much material.

W.P M K

University of Toronto,
Toronto
14th June, 1921

TABLE OF CASES.

THE NATURE OF CANADIAN FEDERALISM

Suggestions looking toward some form of union among the provinces of British North America are frequent in Canadian history from 1784, when the idea was first mooted by Lieutenant-Colonel Morse,[1] to the eve of 1867. Little, however, of the nature of the suggested union can be gained from a study of the extant proposals. If we except the abortive Act of Union[2] for Upper and Lower Canada in 1822, no one except Chief Justice Smith seems to have worked out a scheme in any detail,[3] and his proposals are so vague that it is impossible to decide whether he had in mind a legislative union, a confederation, or a federation. John Beverley Robinson[4] desired to unite the provinces by "giving them a common legislature and erecting them into a kingdom." The phrase seems to point to a legislative union, and this assumption is strengthened by the emphasis which Robinson laid on the fact that the new government would be clearly distinguished from the republican institutions of the United States. There was, however, no political discussion, no examination of the nature and essence of the scheme. With Lord Durham we are in a clearer atmosphere, and he at least defines his terms:

> Two kinds of union have been proposed—federal and legislative. By the first the separate Legislature of each Province would be preserved in its present form, and retain almost all its present attributes of internal legislation, the Federal Legislature exercising no power save in those matters which may have been expressly ceded to it by the Constituent Provinces A legislative union would imply a complete incorporation of the Provinces included in it under one Legislature, exercising universal and sole legislative authority over all of them in exactly the same manner as the Parliament legislates alone for the whole of the British Isles[5]

[1] Canadian Archives Report (1884), p iii

[2] Kennedy, *Documents of the Canadian Constitution*, pp 307 ff.

[3] *Ibid.*, pp 203 ff

[4] Quoted in Egerton and Grant, *Canadian Constitutional Development*, p 147 Cf. Sewell and Robinson, *Plan for a General Legislative Union of the British Provinces in North America* (London, 1824)

[5] *Report on the Affairs of British North America* (Montreal, 1839), p 116

By a "federal union" Durham meant the creation of a central government to which the constituent provinces would delegate certain powers. In other words, the national government would be a delegation from the provincial governments for the carrying out of certain specific purposes. Such a conception raises the question, can such a government be called " a *federal* government"? This question must be discussed at this point, because, as will appear later, such a duscussion is germane to any consideration of the debates in the parliament of Canada in 1865.

Without examining the nature of political unions in the ancient world, on which historians and jurists differ, in American history such a union as that proposed by Lord Durham appears to have been called a *confederation*. "The perpetual Confederation" of Massachusetts, Connecticut, Plymouth, and New Haven (1643-1684), and Franklin's "Draft for Union" in 1754, are cases in point.[1] In both cases, the general or national government was a delegate. It existed on sufferance of creating principals. The best illustration, however, is found in the Articles of Confederation proposed in 1777 and ratified in 1781. Owing their immediate origin to the necessity for military union, they have in addition behind them a political philosophy based on experience. The earliest signs of democratic tendencies in North America are to be found in local government. Here was the pregnant school of political training. As a consequence it is not surprising to find a mistrust of a strong central government running through the whole conception of the union. The unifying machinery created for the purposes of the Revolutionary War was not only weak in those aspects known to every school-boy, but was deliberately made a delegation from states which retained, not theoretically but actually, their political sovereignty. A clear-cut relation of principals and delegate was set up, such a scheme of government being known as a *confederation*. In other words and in legal language, the national government was not sovereign, nor was it endowed with plenary powers within its sphere. It was, as Robert Morris, superintendent of finance for the Thirteen Colonies in 1781-1784, said, "A government whose sole authority consists in the power of framing recommendations." When Hamilton proposed the conference at Philadelphia which framed the constitution of the United States, it was with the idea of creating "an adequate federal government". The new government

[1] Macdonald, *Select Charters*, vol. I, pp. 94 ff.

which took the place of that under the Articles of Confederation was not the agent of the states. It springs, in theory and in statement at least, from the people, and over them within its sphere it has sovereign and plenary power. Allowing that the convention was called merely to revise the Confederation and allowing that the general tone of the convention pointed to something quite different from the constitutional theory superficially found in the written document and elaborated by the Supreme Court, the fact remains that the convention created something new—a federation—as James Wilson of Pennsylvania saw at the time[1] This is the view taken of the constitution by the courts. A federation may originate historically in many ways, but once the federation is formed, the current of historical and legal opinion is that the central and the provincial or state governments have co-ordinate authority. Nor does the fact that the powers given to the national government may be specifically enumerated, and the residue of undefined powers reserved to the states or to the people enter into the discussion. To the uncritical student the fact might point to delegation. But a federal government is created for national purposes and for the undertaking of international obligations; and if those purposes are to be carried out and those obligations enforced—as they could not be under a confederation—then the national government must be endowed with the plenitude of sovereignty within its sphere. That sphere may be defined, or implication may widen its definition, because of the "incidental and instrumental powers", as Judge Cooley said, necessary to its effectual functioning, but definition or non-definition is immaterial. Finally, in this connexion, it is significant that, when the Civil War arose to test the nature of the American constitution, the Southern States called themselves "the Confederate States of America" Their actual constitution may not point to either looseness of union or to weakness of cooperation. Military success alone could finally have tested it; but they deliberately chose a name for their political organization pointing to the loosely cemented régime before the creation of the United States, and their army was known as the "Confederate Army" as distinguished from "the Federal Army of the United States."

When we come to consider the unification of the provinces of British North America, the first thing which strikes us in the

[1] Elliot's Debates, I, p 119, II, p 440.

documents is the mixed and confused use of terms. In the confidential memorandum [1] drawn up in 1864, which was the basis for the Coalition Ministry pledged to carry out the unification, "federal principle", "federal union", and "confederation" are all used to describe the political scheme which brought Conservatives and Liberals together. The inexactitude of the phraseology might be put down to lack of political training were it not for the fact that, during the debates[2] on the Quebec Resolutions in the Parliament of Canada in February, 1865, "federation" and "confederation" seem to have been deliberately used to confuse the issue. It is clear that there was a certain amount of *camouflage.* Macdonald's attitude can be judged from two quotations, taken widely apart, from his speech of February 6:

> The Conference having come to the conclusion that a legislative union, pure and simple, was impracticable, our next attempt was to form a government upon federal principles, which would give to the General Government the strength of a legislative and administrative union, while at the same time it preserved that liberty of action for the different Sections which is allowed by a Federal Union.[3]

> We . . . . strengthen the Central Parliament and make the Confederation one people and one government, instead of five peoples and five governments, with merely a point of authority connecting us to a limited and insufficient extent . . . . this is to be one united Province with the Local Governments and Legislatures subordinate to the General Government and Legislature . . . .[4]

In the first quotation, "federal" is used when the "liberty" of the provinces is referred to; in the second, "confederation"—the designation historically connected with loosely organized unions—is used, when the real nature of Macdonald's proposal is referred to That real nature was nothing else than a thinly-veiled legislative union—a "federation" or a "confederation" (Macdonald did not care what it was called)—in which the provinces should be merely municipal agents of the national government. It is not without significance that in the title of the official debates

[1] Pope, *Memoirs of Sir John A. Macdonald*, vol I, p. 344.

[2] *Parliamentary Debates on the Subject of the Confederation of the British North American Provinces* (Quebec, 1865).

[3] *Ibid*, p 32

[4] *Ibid*, pp 41 ff

the word "Confederation" appears. The object was to carry the proposals. It remained for the astute mind of Antoine Dorion to challenge the ambiguities:

> The Confederation I advocated was a real confederation giving the largest powers to the Local Governments and merely a delegated authority to the General Government—in that respect differing *in toto* from the one now proposed, which gives all the powers to the Central Government and reserves for the Local Governments the smallest possible amount of freedom of action.[1]

Dorion's clearness may have influenced the official title, and it cannot have been entirely an accident that during the ministry of Sir Wilfrid Laurier, who himself came from Dorion's *cénacle*, provincial legislation was largely free from Dominion interference, a matter to which I shall return later in another connexion.

For many years after 1867 the provinces held a subordinate position, as Dorion feared. Until the advent to power of the Liberal party in 1896, "provincial rights" had a small place in Conservative policy, dominated as it was by the personality or memory of Macdonald. But, however much party politics may have forced issues in constitutional law—a matter with which we have no concern—there was a safeguard independent of politics, of the opinions expressed or implied by the Fathers of Canadian unification, and of the fact that they had to be content with an agreement which was but a skeleton and could not embody Macdonald's real aims if it were to be accepted by the provinces. That safeguard is found in the fact that the Privy Council has always considered the *British North America Act* as a British statute, has held that its interpretation must begin from that point of view, and that all its parts must be given their natural sense when read in conjunction. As a consequence, and without for the moment considering the light which that interpretation has thrown on the nature of the Canadian constitution, we have been saved from much emotional challenge, from the so-called invasion of sacrosanct instruments, and from any attempt to confine interpretations within a preconceived Canadian notion of the essence of the Canadian system. These facts are neither academic nor legal. They are of practical importance. Canada has accepted the principle:[2] but it has been rejected by the High Court of Australia, of which the majority tends to believe in the

[1] *Ibid.*, p. 250

[2] *Abbott* v. *City of St John*, 40 Supreme Court of Canada Reports, 597.

immunity of instrumentalities. There are thus grave clashes of interpretation, because the Australian High Court maintains that the Australian constitution cannot be subject to the ordinary rules governing a British statute, which must be modified by the conception of the constitution in the minds of the founders of the Commonwealth.

The almost necessarily incomplete nature of the *British North America Act* has resulted in a series of legal decisions on which it is possible to found some idea of the nature of Canadian federalism. First of all, the Dominion parliament is not a delegation from the imperial parliament or from the provinces.[1] It has full and complete powers within its reference. Secondly, the provincial parliaments are not delegations from the imperial parliament:

> When the British North America Act enacted that there should be a Legislature for Ontario and that its Legislative Assembly should have exclusive authority to make laws for the Province and for provincial purposes in relation to the matters enumerated in Sect. 92, it conferred powers not in any sense to be exercised by delegation from or as agents of the Imperial Parliament, but authority as plenary and as ample within the limits prescribed by Sect. 92 as the Imperial Parliament in the plenitude of its power possessed and could bestow. Within these limits of subjects and area, the local Legislature is supreme and has the same authority as the Imperial Parliament or the Parliament of the Dominion.[2]

Thirdly, the provincial parliaments are not delegations from the Dominion parliament:

> The Provincial Legislature of New Brunswick . . . . derives no authority from the Government of Canada, and its status is in no way analogous to a municipal institution, which is an authority constituted for purposes of local administration. It possesses powers not of administration merely, but of legislation, in the strictest sense of that word; and, within the limits assigned by S. 92 of the Act of 1867, these powers are exclusive and supreme.[3]

From these interpretations it is clear (1) that the Dominion parliament is a sovereign parliament within the meaning of S. 91

[1] *The Attorney General for Canada* v. *Cain and Gilhula*, A. C. 542.

[2] *Hodge* v. *The Queen*, 9 App. Cases, 117.

[3] *The Liquidators of the Maritime Bank of Canada* v. *The Receiver General of New Brunswick* (1892), A. C. 437.

of the Act of 1867; and in no sense a delegate, related to the provinces as principals; (2) that the provincial parliaments are in no sense delegates either of the imperial parliament or of the Dominion parliament.

Further light is thrown on the matter by a famous passage in the judgment delivered by Lord Watson in the last case:

> The Act of 1867 . . . nowhere professes to curtail in any respect the rights and privileges of the Crown or to disturb the relations then subsisting between the Sovereign and the Provinces. The object of the Act was neither to weld the Provinces into one, nor to subordinate Provincial Governments to a central authority, but to create a Federal Government in which they should all be represented, entrusted with the exclusive administration of affairs in which they had a common interest, each Province retaining its independence and autonomy . . As regards those matters which by S. 92 are specially reserved for provincial legislation, the legislation of each Province continues . . . as supreme as it was before the passing of the Act.

A fourth conclusion emerges. The provinces remain "independent and autonomous". They have not been destroyed. They possess the executive power "before Confederation minus the powers surrendered at Confederation".[1] In all these cases the court did not discuss the nature of that surrender. It accepted the fact. It interpreted that fact, however, in the sense of a *federation* and not of a *confederation*. The conclusion we can come to seems to be that Canada is a federation in essence; that is, that the central national government is in no sense a delegation; that the provincial governments are in no sense "municipal"; and that national and local governments exercise coordinate authority and are severally sovereign within the sphere specifically or generically or by implication constitutionally granted to them. This construction agrees with the preamble of the *British North America Act*, "Whereas the Provinces of Canada, Nova Scotia and New Brunswick have expressed their desire to be federally united," however loosely that preamble may originally have been constructed; and it seems to override any idea that Canada is a confederation. In the incidences of construction—to which I shall return—the federal conception may not be complete, but the essence seems to be established.

[1] Keith, *Responsible Government in the Dominions*, I, p 124.

Unfortunately, however, in an Australian case[1] before the Judicial Committee of the Privy Council in 1914, Lord Haldane made some remarks which appear to contradict views previously laid down and to re-open the whole question. It is well to quote him at length. During the pleadings he said:

> With deference to a great many people who talk on platforms just now of the "Federal System", in Canada there is no federal system. What happened was this: An Act was passed in 1867 which made a new start and divided certain powers of government, some being given to the Parliament of Canada, and some to the Parliament of the Provinces. The Provinces were created *de novo*. The Provinces did not come together and make a federal arrangement under which they retained their existing powers and parted with certain of them and an Imperial Statute has got to ratify the bargain; on the contrary the whole vitality and ambit of the Canadian Constitution was a surrender, if you like, first, and then devolution . . . The meaning of a federal government is that a number of States come together and put certain of their powers into common custody, and that is the Federal Constitution in Australia, but in Canada not at all.[2]

In the judgment he said:

> But there remains a question which goes to the root of the controversy between the parties Were the Royal Commissions Acts *intra vires* of the Commonwealth Parliament? This is a question which can only be answered by examining the scheme of the Act of 1900, which established the Commonwealth Constitution. About the fundamental principle of that Constitution there can be no doubt. It is federal in the strict sense of the term, as a reference to what was established on a different footing in Canada shows. The *British North America Act* of 1867 commences with a preamble that the then Provinces have expressed their desire to be federally united into one Dominion with a Constitution similar in principle to that of the United Kingdom. In a loose sense the word "federal" may be used, as it is there used, to describe any arrangement under which self-contained states agree to delegate their powers to a Common Government with a view to entirely new constitutions, even of the States themselves. But the natural and literal interpretation of the word confines its application to cases in which these

[1] *Attorney General for the Commonwealth of Australia* v. *Colonial Sugar Refining Co., Ltd* (1914) A C 237

[2] *Times Law Reports*, XXX, p 205

> States while agreeing on a measure of delegation, yet in the main continue to preserve their original Constitutions. Now, as regards Canada, the second of the Resolutions passed at Quebec in 1864, on which the British North America Act was founded, shows that what was in the minds of those who agreed on the Resolutions was a general Government charged with matters of common interest, and new and merely local Governments for the Provinces. The Provinces were to have fresh and much restricted Constitutions, their Governments being entirely remodelled. This plan was carried out by the Imperial Statute of 1867 By 91st Section a general power was given to the new Parliament of Canada to make laws for the peace, order and good government of Canada without restriction to specific subject, and excepting only the subjects specifically and exclusively assigned to the Provincial Legislatures by S 92 There followed an enumeration of subjects which were to be dealt with by the Dominion Parliament, but this enumeration was not to restrict the generality of the power conferred on it. The Act, therefore, departs widely from the true federal model adopted in the Constitution of the United States, the tenth Amendment to which declares that the powers not delegated to the United States by the Constitution, nor prohibited to it by the States are reserved to the States respectively, or to their people. Of the Canadian Constitution the true view appears, therefore, to be that, although it was founded on the Quebec Resolutions and so must be accepted as a treaty of union among these Provinces, yet when once enacted by the Imperial Parliament, it constituted a fresh departure, and established new Dominion and Provincial Governments with defined powers and duties both derived from the Act of the Imperial Parliament which was their legal source.

Lord Haldane's statements can be broken up and considered under several heads. First, he defines a federal state as one in which "States while agreeing to a measure of delegation yet in the main continue to preserve their original Constitutions"—"a federal arrangement under which they retained their existing powers and parted with certain of them". It cannot but be a surprise to constitutional students to find a federal constitution defined as one in which the central or national government is a delegation from the constituent states or provinces. I believe that Lord Haldane's definition is based on an entirely wrong view of the essence of a federation, and that he has confused a federation with a confederation. Secondly, it need not be denied that a federation may originate as he suggests; but it is surely illogical to confuse a constitution with the historical processes by which it originated. Lord Haldane would have us assume that unless certain antecedent procedure takes place it is improper to describe the result as a federal state. Such a position cannot seriously be maintained. Political definitions must be confined to facts as they are, and must not be made meaningless by the dead hand of historical or social movements out of which the facts grew. Thirdly, he cites the United States as a true type of federation because it fulfills his processes. It is obvious to ask, is the United States no longer federal because it has admitted to the original "measure of delegation" new states other than the original colonies which alone were parties to the original "federal agreement"? Would Lord Haldane have us believe that the admission of newer states, which made no pact, has destroyed the federal character of the American constitution? Finally his history of the formation of the Canadian constitution is too partial and incomplete to be entirely true. If we concede that old rights were entirely surrendered, and that their retention, minus those conceded to the national government, is necessary to a federal union, then we have no federation in Canada. But it is impossible to make this a rule of constitutional law. In the Dominion the provinces were not formed *de novo*. Canada was divided and the executive authority was maintained in the divisions expressly by the Act of 1867, subject to those changes necessary for the general union. The constitutions of New Brunswick and Nova Scotia were also, subject to the provisions of the Act, continued as they existed at the Union.[1] It was doubtless with these sections in mind that Lord Watson laid down the principle already quoted,[2] which is completely at variance with Lord Haldane's opinion. Lord Watson's conception has been acted on to such an extent that to abandon it would upset much of the structure of the constitution. It has established the generally accepted theory that Canada is a federation in which sovereign power is divided among co-ordinate governments, none of which are delegations and among which the provincial governments are not new creations, but retain "their independence and autonomy".

The real questions to decide, shorn of all theories, are these: Are the national and provincial governments related to one another as principal or delegate? What is the real and precise

[1] B.N.A. Act, §§ 64, 65, 88
[2] *Supra*, p. 7

nature of the authority which they may exercise within their spheres? We have seen that it has been laid down that the various parliaments in Canada are sovereign within the orbit of their established jurisdictions, and that they compel obedience as such. Lord Haldane's opinions, therefore, cannot be accepted as overthrowing the federal essence of the Canadian constitution.

When we come, however, to consider some particular features of the constitution—the Canadian Senate, the office of the Lieutenant-governor, and the Dominion power of disallowing provincial Acts—we may find modifications in the actual working of the federal idea, which yet do not destroy the essence. There is evidence, too, of tendencies to bring these features into accordance with the federal idea.

It must at once be conceded that the Canadian Senate is not the product of a single and intelligible political principle. Indeed, it attempts to embody two ideas—nomination by the Crown, and a timid hankering after representation of grouped provinces. It may be that this attempt has caused it to become almost "a cipher" surrounded "with derisive state" and "the trappings of impotence";[1] but once an elective second chamber was ruled out of the range of possibilities, if federation were to take place, and once the constituent provinces decided on the necessity of a second chamber,[2] it is hard to see how the Senate could have embodied the single federal principle. On the other hand, Macdonald went out of his way to emphasize how, even with nomination, the provinces would be protected: "In order to protect local interests and to prevent sectional jealousies, it was found necessary that the three great divisions into which British North America is separated should be represented in the Upper House on the principle of equality."[3] With temporary obscurity, into which we need not here enter,[4] this plan has been adhered to, and in 1915 when a reconstruction of the Senate was necessary for political and geographical reasons, the Dominion parliament accepted the principle and it was embodied in an imperial Act.[5]

To Macdonald's prophecy, however, of the impossibility of the senate being filled with "partisans and political supporters",[6]

[1] Goldwin Smith, *Canada and the Canadian Question* (1891), p 164.
[2] *Confederation Debates*, pp 34 ff
[3] Cf. B.N A Act, §§ 21, 22
[4] Keith, *Imperial Unity and the Dominions*, pp 394 ff.
[5] *Parliamentary Papers*, Cd 7897: 5 and 6 George V c. 45 (Imp Act).
[6] Kennedy, *op. cit*, p 609

his own political life gave the initial lie. Dorion and Dunkin saw the party possibilities and the weakness in construction. The latter also made an interesting forecast:

> I think I can defy them to show that the Cabinet can be formed on any other principle than that of a representation of the several Provinces in that Cabinet, for it is admitted that the Provinces are not really represented to any federal intent in the Legislative Council [i e. the Senate]. The Cabinet here must discharge all that kind of function, which in the United States is performed, in the federal sense, by the Senate. And precisely as in the United States, wherever a federal check is needed, the Senate has to do federal duty as an integral part of the Executive Government. So here, when that check cannot be so got, we must seek such substitute for it as we may in a federal composition of the Executive Council [i.e. the Cabinet]; that is to say, by making it distinctly representative of the Provinces [1]

While Dunkin's fears that the cabinet would be weakened by sectional differences, and by rendering insecure the constitutional principle of united cabinet responsibility, have not been realized, yet he foretold what has become an interesting federal by-product in Canada, most federal cabinets being formed, as far as possible, on a recognition of the claims of the constituent provinces.[2] On the other hand, it is not uninteresting to note that in the midst of many suggestions for reform, if not abolition of the Senate, the quasi-federal aspect has not been obscured. Sir George Ross, for example, maintains that "the first and only duty of the Senate is to consider the treaty rights of all the Provinces under the Constitution".[3]

When we come to consider the Dominion power[4] of appointing the lieutenant-governors of the provinces and of disallowing provincial Acts in relation to the nature of Canadian federalism, we approach a problem to which no adequate consideration can be given here. The difficulty is as old as federation. On the one hand Macdonald in 1865 emphasized the necessity "that the chief executive officer in each of the Provinces must be subordinate", because the intention was to create subordinate local governments and legislatures. Dorion saw here the negation of any such

[1] *Confederation Debates*, p 497.

[2] Porritt, *Evolution of the Dominion of Canada*, pp. 357 ff. Cf. Laurier's opinions on the principle, *House of Commons Debates*, May 15, 1909

[3] Ross, *The Senate of Canada* (1914), p. 51.

[4] B N A Act, §§ 56, 58, 90.

thing as responsible provincial government, while Dunkin found in the provision for disallowance the impossibility of any real provincial autonomy.[1]

Before attempting to consider the question, it is well to recall that Hamilton, who may be said to have originated the federal as opposed to the confederate constitution of the Thirteen Colonies, deliberately proposed at the Philadelphia Convention that the President should appoint the Governors of the various States, and that he should have an absolute veto on the Acts of the State Legislatures.[2] Diplomatic reasons prevented the suggestion from being incorporated in the constitution, but it is important to note that no one considered it opposed to the essence of a federal constitution, least of all Hamilton, who had the clearest conception of the nature of a federation The power, at least over state legislation, was soon vested in the Supreme Court.[3]

It is unnecessary to linger over questions raised concerning the appointment of the lieutenant-governors. Two of them have been dismissed in Canadian history since Federation by the governor-general, and at first there was a general disposition to consider them mere creatures of the Dominion government. That view has been entirely abandoned. The method of their appointment is evidence of the federal link; but it has been decided that they possess in full the provincial executive authority,[4] that there is no constitutional anomaly in their appointment, and that when once appointed they are as much representatives of the Crown for every purpose of government in the provinces as the governor-general is for all purposes of Dominion government [5]

The Dominion power of disallowance is of more vital interest.[6] The governor-general on the advice of responsible ministers (in this case, the federal minister of justice) has the power to disallow a provincial Act within one year after the receipt of the Act from the lieutenant-governor of a province. We can well understand a principle of disallowance where a constitutional question arises; but it would be safer if the decision in such cases were left

[1] *Confederation Debates*, pp 42, 225, 502

[2] Elliot's Debates, V, App 5

[3] *Statutes at Large* (U S A), I, September 24, 1789

[4] *The Attorney General of Ontario* v *Mercer*, 8, App Cas 767.

[5] *The Liquidators of the Maritime Bank of Canada*, v. *The Receiver-General of New Brunswick* (1892), A C. 437.

[6] See in detail Keith, *Responsible Government*, II, pp 725 ff , *Imperial Unity*, pp. 432 ff ; Lefroy, *Canada's Federal System*, I, pp. 30-34, 42-46.

to the courts as in the United States, since in a federation differences on constitutional law must frequently arise. The resolution of the problem of *intra vires* or *ultra vires* ought not to be left to the minister of justice. This tends to make him too supreme, and to detract from the character of the Supreme Court of Canada or of the Privy Council[1]. For many years, however, after 1867 the Dominion government considered it was justified in disallowing provincial Acts which appeared unjust or oppressive—through, for example, interference with vested rights without compensation, or through the impairing of contractual obligations. Provincial Acts were disallowed under these principles.

It appears early to have been a working convention of the Canadian constitution that, as the courts would deal with legislation *ultra vires* of the provinces, the power of disallowance was intended to cover cases outside legal review. In other words, the power of disallowance was inserted in the *British North America Act* to cover, in general terms, unjust, confiscatory or *ex post facto* legislation, against which there are express safeguards in the constitution of the United States.

A priori, there is a certain amount of support for this contention. It is well known that the constitution of the United States was carefully studied by those who laid the foundations and organized the framework of Canadian federation. It is not unreasonable to suppose that they had in mind in the "disallowance sections" a means of dealing with provincial legislation which might be judged unsound in principle. Cartier, as we shall see, explicitly said that this was the intention. As a matter of fact, from federation to 1893, the weight of evidence, both from the bench and from the federal cabinet, is in favour of this point of view.

On the judicial side there are opinions from Justices Ramsay, Strong, and Chief Justice Draper which can be summarized in the words of the latter: "The Governor-General . . . is entrusted

[1] See a protest in these terms from the government of British Columbia, August 22, 1905, *Provincial Legislation, 1904-1906* (Ottawa, 1907), pp. 148 ff.:—"The effect of disallowance . . . is to make the Minister of Justice the highest judicial dignitary in the land for the determination of constitutional questions, and in reality above the Supreme Court of Canada. The decisions of the Supreme Court of Canada are open to question in the Judicial Committee of the Privy Council. From the decision of the Minister of Justice there is no appeal. He stands alone."

with authority, to which a corresponding duty attaches, to disallow any law contrary to reason, or to natural justice, or equity."[1] The opinions from the Canadian executive can be summarized in chronological order and are found under date in the various Reports of the federal ministers of justice.[2]

First, there is the general Report of Sir J. A. Macdonald (1 July 1867-6 Nov. 1873)[3] dated 8 June 1868. He recommends that the minister of justice should report on provincial Acts basing his reports on one or all of four heads (*a*) as being altogether illegal or unconstitutional, (*b*) as being illegal or unconstitutional in part, (*c*) as clashing in cases of concurrent jurisdiction, with federal legislation, (*d*) as affecting the interest of the Dominion as a whole. This general scheme has been claimed to support, on the one hand, the contention that nothing is said concerning unjust or unsound legislation, and, on the other hand, to include it under the general term "illegal," which appears to be distinguished from "unconstitutional." Up to 1896, the latter contention seems largely to have held the field Unjust or unsound legislation figured with unconstitutional reasons and reasons based on general federal policy in the disallowance of provincial Acts.

In 1871 Sir J. A. Macdonald disallowed a railway Act of the the province of Manitoba because "no sufficient provision was made for compensation for any infringement of the rights of property or other vested rights."

In 1874 the lieutenant-governor of Prince Edward Island reserved "The Land Purchase Act, 1874" for the governor-general's pleasure on the grounds that it was subversive of the rights of property, ruinous to the proprietors and a dangerous precedent. It was disallowed for the above reasons, and because the arbitration was arbitrary and made no provision against impartiality and for speedy settlement. The report was presented by the deputy-minister, and the minister of justice, Hon. Télesphore Fournier (8 July 1874-18 May 1875), concurred.

In 1874, a Manitoba Act was disallowed by Sir A. A. Dorion (7 Nov. 1873-1 June 1874) because it might tend to interfere with the survey of public lands.

[1]See Ramsay, J , in *Angers* v. *Queen Insurance Co* , 22 L C J , and *Corporation of Three Rivers* v. *Sulte*, 5 L N. Strong, J , in *Severn* v *The Queen*, 2 S C R Draper, C.J , in *re Goodhue*, 19 Grant For a direct opposite opinion, however, see Casault, J , in *Guay* v. *Blanchet*, 5 Q.L R. (1879)

[2]Hodgins, *Dominion and Provincial Legislation*, 1867, ff

[3]The dates in brackets refer to the term of office as minister of justice

In 1876, an Act of the legislature of Prince Edward Island was disallowed by Hon. R. Scott, acting-minister of justice, because it dealt with the rights of parties then under or subject to litigation under the Act which it proposed to amend, and because there was no provision saving the rights and proceedings of such persons.

In 1881, the Ontario legislature passed an Act granting all persons rights to use improvements for purposes of floating down logs on payment of a reasonable toll. An appeal was made to the governor-general for disallowance on the grounds of being unconstitutional, of depriving the petitioner of private rights, of being *ex post facto*. The Act was disallowed because it seemed "to take away the use of the owner's property and give it to another," and because, assuming that the local legislature had such a power,

> "It devolves upon the Dominion government to see that such power is not exercised in flagrant violation of private rights and natural justice, especially when, as in this case, in addition to interfering with private rights in the way alluded to, the act overrides a decision of a court of competent jurisdiction by declaring retrospectively that the law always was, and is, different from that laid down by the court."

(Hon. J. Macdonald, 17 Oct. 1878-20 May 1881). Ontario objected in strong terms against any review of a provincial Act *inter vires* of the province, and reënacted the Act of 1881, only to have it again disallowed by the Dominion.

In 1887, Manitoba passed an Act providing that every person connected with any public work should be deemed a servant of the Crown, and that the sanction of the minister of public works should be deemed in the courts of justice full and competent authority and justification for any work done with the approval and on behalf of such minister. Sir J. A. Macdonald, for the minister of justice, recommended disallowance, because the immunity from liabilities and responsibilities was of an unreal and extraordinary character and manifestly interfered with private rights.

In 1888, New Brunswick passed an Act which appeared to give a new company rights inconsistent with rights granted to a Dominion company. Petitioners claimed that their charter had been ratified by the province, that no cause was shown for forfeiture of their charter, and that proprietary and contractural rights were violated. Sir J. S. D. Thompson (25 Sept. 1885-

12 Dec. 1894) recommended disallowance, because the Act interfered with and restricted a Dominion Act, and because it diminished the value of franchises already granted.

In 1888, Quebec passed an Act to enable the province to issue debentures for the purpose of redeeming outstanding liabilities and to save the amount of interest paid yearly by the province. Sir John Thompson observed that the Act authorized the province to violate contracts without compensation, that it would affect the credit of the province and might indicate the possibility that faith might not be kept inviolate between the province and its creditors, and that it might hurt the other provinces. Quebec undertook to repeal the objectionable sections.

In the same year, a Manitoba Act was amended on suggestion from the Dominion, in order not to affect prejudicially the credit of the municipalities of the province.

In 1889, the legislature of New Brunswick passed an Act forfeiting mining leases under conditions set out in the act. Sir John Thompson characterized the act as

> "Seeming to be at variance with the principles of justice and to invade the rights of property which it is so important to preserve for the credit of the whole country and for the safety of private persons. If it is desirable that a province should resume any part of its patrimony, the methods adopted should be those which recognize and provide for the rights which have accrued under the sanction of the Crown."

He recommended amendment to remove such objectionable features as he enumerated. Shortly afterwards the same minister of justice recommended the province of Quebec so to amend a mining law of 1890 as to remove "any objection to the Act on the ground of its being a confiscation of existing private rights as claimed by the petitioners." He also brought about the amendment of a Nova Scotia Act of 1892 because it prejudiced rights under litigation. In 1893 an Ontario Act occasioned the federal criticism that a statute which interfered with vested rights of property or with the obligations of contracts without compensation ought to come within the Dominion sphere of disallowance.

Thompson, however, in 1886 and in 1888 seems to have deviated from his general principles. Once he refused to consider the question whether an Act was just or unjust, seeing that it was undoubtedly *intra vires* of the province; and once, while pronouncing the legislation under consideration as pernicious, he refused to recommend disallowance because it did not affect the interests of the Dominion. The Hon. Edward Blake (19 May 1875-8 June 1877), in refusing a petition against an Ontario statute (38 Vict. c. 75), said that he did not conceive that he was called upon "to express an opinion upon the allegations of the petition as to the injustice alleged to be effected by the Act. This was a matter for the local legislature".[1]

These three opinions are more or less isolated in the years 1867-1893. Whatever other motives—if any—which may have been at work during that period, it is clear that there is a certain consistency of purpose in dealing with provincial legislation which appeared to hurt private property, to invalidate contracts or to be contrary to what were known as "sound principles of legislation." It lies outside the discussion to search for or to examine motives which political writers have suggested. All that can be said here is that the constitutional power of disallowance was consistently used during these years to protect those spheres of provincial civil life, which are protected explicitly or by implication in the constitution of the United States.

From 1893 on to Mr. Doherty's instance of disallowance in 1918, we see a new principle at work which is largely an extension of the idea formulated by Blake. It is not uninteresting to note that this new principle runs parallel with the definitions of Canadian federalism which have already been considered. It is true that the *dicta* in *Hodge* v. *The Queen* are older; but Lord Watson's *dicta* were uttered in 1892. In *Brophy* v. *Attorney-General of Manitoba* in 1895 Lord Herschell said:

> "In relation to the subjects specified in sec. 92 of the British North America Act and not falling within those set forth in sec. 91, the exclusive powers of the provincial legislatures may be said to be absolute."[2]

Three years later he said:

> "The suggestion that the power might be abused so as to amount to a practical confiscation of property does not warrant the imposition by the courts of any limit upon the absolute power of legislation conferred. The supreme legislative power in relation to any subject matter is always capable of abuse, but it is not to be assumed that it

[1]Cf. Blake's opinion, however, on a Quebec statute (38 Vict c 17) in 1876, which differs somewhat from that referred to above

[2]A. C. [1895], 202.

will be improperly used; if it is, the only remedy is an appeal to those by whom the Legislature is elected.[1]

This period was the golden age of provincial rights, when the Privy Council was gradually bringing to light the essentially federal nature of the Canadian constitution. Indeed, the new era in the sphere of Dominion disallowance is almost ushered in by a federal minister of justice relying on Lord Herschell's words in the last case to which I have referred.

Indirectly, in 1898, the provinces of Canada received support from a despatch from the Hon. Joseph Chamberlain to the Governor of Newfoundland refusing to disallow a Newfoundland Act. It is true that the despatch deals with the imperial power of the exercise of disallowance in relation to legislation of a self-governing Dominion; but the principles involved are common to those just considered. There is no imperial issue brought forward: "it is nowhere alleged that the interests of any other part of the Empire are involved or that the Act is in any way repugnant to Imperial Legislation." The Act dealt with financial and administrative matters of a local nature. Disputes in that connection must be settled locally. Where disallowance was claimed on account of policy, Mr. Chamberlain would not consider the claim. The whole tenor of the despatch lies in the idea that, granted the constitutional power to legislate, and granted that imperial policy is not involved, to disallow would be to negative self-government:

> "My action has throughout been governed by constitutional principles, on which I am bound to act; and I think it is desirable that it should be made quite clear that in accepting the privilege of self-government, the Colony has accepted the full responsibilities inseparable from that privilege, and that if the machinery it has provided for the work of legislation and administration has proved defective, or the persons to whom it has entrusted its destinies have failed to discharge their trust, they cannot look to Her Majesty's Government to supplement or remedy these defects, or to judge between them and their duly chosen representatives."[2]

The despatch touches hands with Edward Blake and with the *dicta* of the Judicial Committee of the Privy Council. If a

[1]*Attorney General for Canada* v. *Attorney General for the Provinces of Ontario, etc.*, [1898]. A.C. 700 (The Fisheries' Case).

[2] Despatch of 5 December 1898, *Parliamentary Papers*, C. 8137. Cf. *London Times*, 23 January, 1899.

province has self-government, if no Dominion interests or policies are violated, if the legislation is constitutionally *intra vires*, then the people cannot expect redress and it ought not to be given, if such legislation appears unjust. The remedy lies in their gift of responsible and representative government.

When we resume the consideration of disallowance we almost at once see the true federal idea at work. In 1897 Sir Oliver Mowat (13 July 1896–17 Nov. 1897) laid it down that it was none of his business as minister of justice to review a provincial Act because of injustice. In 1898 the Hon. David Mills (18 Nov. 1897-7 Feb. 1902) based his refusal to disallow on the passage already quoted from the Fisheries' Case. In 1900, we see the influence of Mr. Chamberlain's despatch in a letter which Mr. Mills addressed to the premier of Ontario. He says that he will interfere, where it is clear that a well defined Dominion policy is endangered by provincial legislation. It is fair to add that he disallowed in 1898 a Yukon Ordinance which unjustly discriminated against certain classes of citizens. There is a difference, however, between the organization of the Yukon and the older provinces and Mr. Mills' more constant opinion is found in his report of 31 December 1901 in relation to a British Columbia statute:

> "Your Excellency's Government is not in any wise responsible for the principle of the legislation, and, as has been already stated in this report with regard to an Ontario statute, the proper remedy in such cases lies with the Legislature or its constitutional judges."

Sir Charles Fitzpatrick (11 Feb. 1902-4 June 1906) followed Mr. Mills. He did not conceal his dislike for legislation which diminished or affected existing rights, but he concluded that

> "There is a difficulty about Your Excellency-in-Council giving relief in such cases without affirming a policy which requires Your Excellency's government to put itself to a large extent in the place of the legislature and to judge of the propriety of its acts relative to matters committed by the constitution to the exclusive legislative authority of the province"

This opinion brings the history down to the regime of Sir Allen Aylesworth (4 June 1906-6 Oct. 1911).

Protests from the provinces forced the federal government to reconsider its position, especially as they emphasized the fact that local autonomy was apparently insecure, even in spheres where the provinces claimed exclusive jurisdiction. In 1908, Sir Allen

Aylesworth, then minister of justice, made a Report, which was approved by the governor-general, in which he said.

> It is not intended by the *British North America Act* that the power of disallowance shall be exercised for the purpose of annulling Provincial Legislation even though your Excellency's Ministers consider the Legislation unjust, or oppressive, or in conflict with recognized legal principles, so long as such Legislation is within the power of the Provincial Legislature to enact it [1]

In 1912, however, on two occasions[2] the present minister of justice, Mr. Doherty, while refusing to disallow for reasons stated, claimed that he entertained no doubt

> That the power is constitutionally capable of exercise, and may on occasion be properly invoked, for the purpose of preventing, not inconsistently with the public interest, irreparable injustice or undue interference with private rights or property through the operation of local Statutes *intra vires* of the Legislatures.

On May 30, 1918, Mr. Doherty disallowed, with the approval of the governor-general, an Act of the British Columbia legislature (7-8 George V. c. 71), because it diminished substantially the consideration of a contract. He did this after hearing an argument before the Dominion prime minister, the minister of public works and himself, and after notifying the attorney-general for British Columbia and hearing counsel for the petitioners. There are two passages in this Report[3] which deserve attention. Firstly, Mr Doherty lays it down that he does not consider the Dominion veto obsolete in cases where hardship, inequality, injustice, interference with vested rights or contracts are brought forward. While preferring as a rule to leave such cases, where the legislation is *intra vires* of the province, to be redressed by the local legislature, yet he maintains that there are "principles governing the exercise of legislative power other than the mere respect and deference due to the expression of the will of the local constituent Assembly, which must be considered in the exercise of the prerogative of disallowance." He refuses to lay down those principles or to formulate general rules, but he suggests that "interference with vested rights or the obligation of Contracts except for public purposes, and upon due indemnity are processes of legislation which do not appear

[1] *Provincial Legislation, 1904-1906*, p. 8.

[2] Lefroy, *Treatise on Canadian Constitutional Law*, pp 63-64, 172, n. 47.

[3] P. C (May 30, 1918), 1334.

just or desirable." Secondly, upon the submission of the attorney-general for British Columbia that disallowance would involve a serious interference with provincial rights, he says:

> Provincial rights are conferred and limited by the *British North America Act*, and while the Provinces have the right to legislate upon the subjects committed to their legislative authority, the power to disallow any such legislation is conferred by the same constitutional instrument upon the Governor-General in Council, and incident to the power is the duty to exercise it in proper cases. This power and the correspondent duty are conferred for the benefit of the Provinces as well as for that of the Dominion at large . . The mere execution of the power of disallowance does not therefore conflict with Provincial rights, although doubtless the responsibility for the exercise of the power which rests with Your Excellency in Council ought to be so regulated as not to be made effective except in those cases in which, as in the present case, the propriety of exercising the power is demonstrated.

This opinion is in direct contrast with that expressed by Sir Allen Aylesworth, and thus elaborated by him in the House of Commons:

> I was not, as advising His Excellency in Council, called upon to think at all of the injustice, of the outrageous character, it might be, of the Legislation; but . . . my one inquiry ought to be whether or not there was anything in the legislation itself which went beyond the power of the Provincial Legislature

Sir Allen Aylesworth considered that the provincial legislatures within the scope of their jurisdictions were on an absolutely level footing with the parliament of Canada, and that protest against such provincial legislation as was under consideration ought to be fought out at the Provincial polls, as must be done in case of similar Dominion legislation [1]

In December, 1909, a similar line was taken by the province of Ontario. The Ontario government conceded, as it was compelled to do, the right to disallow, but it maintained that that right was technical and must be judged in conjunction with the interpretation of the *British North America Act*, as a whole, which gave to the provincial governments sovereign powers within their jurisdictions. Any other view would mean that the people

[1] *House of Commons Debates* (1909), pp 1750 ff Cf. Mr Justice Riddell in *Smith* v *City of London* (20 Ont Law Reports 1909, 133) "An Act of Parliament can do no wrong, though it may do several things that look pretty odd."

of the provinces had not the full enjoyment of their civil rights with reference to those subjects within their well-defined jurisdiction.[1]

The divergence of opinion is not one merely between two ministers of justice. Professor Lefroy, with a strong catena of cases behind him, maintained that the courts could not disallow a Dominion or provincial Act "merely because it may affect injuriously private rights, or destroy vested rights or be otherwise unjust or contrary to sound principles of legislature".[2] Mr. Justice Riddell, in a famous judgment, lays down the principle that

> The Legislature within its jurisdiction can do everything which is not naturally impossible, and is restrained by no rule human or divine ... The prohibition "Thou shalt not steal" has no legal force upon the sovereign body, and there would be no necessity for compensation to be given [3]

The Courts may, and often must, determine whether or not any Act is constitutional; but once a decision is arrived at establishing the right of a province to legislate on the subject matter of the Act "arguments founded on alleged hardship or injustice can have no weight".[4]

On the one hand is the opinion which holds that the provinces of Canada are sovereign within their established spheres, and that a Court, and *a fortiori* the Dominion cabinet, ought not to disallow a provincial Act except when it is clearly unconstitutional. On the other hand is the opinion which holds that the Dominion cabinet can veto a provincial Act, otherwise *intra vires*, when it comes within such description as that made by Mr. Doherty or Professor Lefroy.

Lay opinion is of little worth, but certain criticisms can be submitted. If the constitution is "similar in principle to that of the United Kingdom"[5] and if the provincial legislatures are in reality what the Privy Council has already defined them to be—sovereign powers with as full and ample authority as the imperial

[1] Attorney-general of Ontario, to the governor-general of Canada, December 9, 1909.

[2] *Op. cit*, p 70

[3] *Florence Mining Co.* v. *The Cobalt Lake Mining Co* (1909) 18 Ontario Law Reports, 257.

[4] Moss, C. J, in *ibid*, p 293 See, *inter alia*, Mr Justice Riddell's *The Constitution of Canada* and the valuable notes on Chapter III

[5] Cf. Edward Blake "a single line imported into the system that complex and somewhat indefinite aggregate called the British Constitution" (*St Catharines Milling and Lumber Co.* v, *The Queen*, 14 App Cas 46)

parliament within their jurisdictions—certain conclusions seem to follow. The rule of British constitutional law must hold that, granted the legislative power, it is impossible to question the justice of that legislation. This is Mr. Justice Riddell's opinion. Redress lies with the people "who are the best judges of the laws they are governed by".[1] This conception, too, fits in with a federal idea of the nature of Canadian government, suggested, as we have seen, by Lord Watson. Of course, it would not destroy a federal constitution had the Canadian constitution contained a clause like that in the constitution of the United States,[2] prohibiting the provinces from impairing the obligation of contracts or from interfering with matters within Mr. Doherty's description. The suggestion merely is this: once it is clear that the Act is constitutional, then its consequences and results in actual life are open to judgment by the electorate alone.

On the other hand, with due deference and respect, it is submitted that, if Mr. Doherty's position is the correct one, then the federal idea is overthrown, for the legislatures of the provinces cease to be the bodies described by the Privy Council and take that subordinate position which Macdonald meant them to hold and Professor Dicey appears to believe they possess.[3] I have not forgotten that it is possible for such Acts as Mr. Doherty has in mind to be drawn into a clearly defined constitutional issue, and disallowed because they may infringe on the Dominion power to legislate for "the peace, order and good government of Canada." That is a matter for interpretation legally constituted, and it does not appear open to the Courts in this connexion "to substitute their own opinion, whether a particular enactment was calculated as a matter of fact and good policy to secure peace, order and good government, for the decision of the Legislature".[4] It is quite a different thing, however, that the supporters of this opinion mean. Again, I would submit that the emphasis laid on this position seems to magnify one power allowed by the *British North America Act* to the Dominion government at the expense of the construction of the Act as a whole and of the general elas-

[1] Riddell, *op cit*, p 98 Mr Justice Riddell's opinion was approved by the Court of Appeal for Ontario and by the Judicial Committee of the Privy Council (*Ibid*, p. 112).

[2] Article I, §§ 10

[3] *Law of the Constitution* (8th Ed), Ch III Cf. Laski, *The Problem of Sovereignty*, pp 267, ff

[4] Keith, *Responsible Government*, I, p 419

ticity of its terms. The difficulty of the position is obvious, but it is interesting to note that Cartier supported Mr. Doherty's point of view:

> The presumption is it [the power of disallowance by the Federal Government] will be exercised in cases of unjust or unwise legislation.

He drew from Dunkin apt criticism:

> The hon. gentleman's presumption reminds me of one perhaps as conclusive, but which Dickens tells us failed to satisfy Mr. Bumble. That henpecked beadle is said to have said, on hearing of the legal presumption that a man's wife acts under his control: "If the law presumes anything of the sort, the law's a fool—a natural fool." If this permission of disallowance rests on a presumption that the legislation of our Provinces is going to be unjust or unwise, it may be needed; but under that idea one might have done better either not to allow, or else to restrict within narrower limits, such legislation. If the promised non-exercise of the power to disallow rests on the presumption that all will be done justly and wisely in the Provincial Legislatures, the legislative power is well given; but, then there is no need, on the other hand, for the permission to disallow.

Dorion, however, with this power of disallowance among other things in his mind, followed with the conclusion that there was "no real autonomy allowed to the Provinces", that "disallowance of all autonomy to the Provinces" characterized the scheme.[1] If that be conceded, the nature of Canadian government is that of a thinly veiled legislative union; and this position is difficult to maintain considering the history, the legal decisions, and the actual results worked out because of them.[2] It challenges the authority of provincial legislation, otherwise sound, and, it is submitted, it re-opens the whole question of local government within any province. If it be correct, it is inevitable that the binding force of local regulations may be disputed on the prin-

[1] *Confederation Debates*, p. 502, Kennedy, *op. cit.*, p. 661.

[2] Cf. Attorney General of British Columbia to the Federal Minister of Justice, December 20, 1901: "In the early days of Confederation the Dominion Executive appear to have been imbued with the notion that the relation between the Dominion and the Provinces was analogous to that existing between parent and child, and to have acted accordingly. That view of the status of the Provinces has been overthrown by a series of Imperial Privy Council decisions which have clearly established that the Provinces acting within the scope of their powers are almost sovereign States." *Provincial Legislation, 1901-1903* (Ottawa, 1905), p. 56.

ciple *delegatus non potest delegare.* Provincial regulations of factories or of public health, for example, may well be called in question by the citizens of a province. And yet this "big County Council"[1]—this province—has the constitutional power to change its own constitution. The two things seem incompatible.

The two well-defined divisions of the subject seem to correspond to two well-defined periods in social development. The first might be called the period of growth. Material development and economic progress are the predominating social characteristics. With their foundations in progress, constitutional issues do not create vital and widespread interests, and much is often conceded, or allowed to go unchallenged, or is consented to "against a day." Thus the Dominion government, with the strong bias lent to the federation by Sir John Macdonald, acquired much actual power. But once the foundations of social progress became secure and economic expansion began to demand such wide securities as its exponents seemed to consider necessary, constitutional challenges become more and more common. The courts were forced to consider the constitution in all its bearings and to give such interpretations to it as were consistent with its construction as a whole. The second period is the period of provincial rights which have increased under judicial interpretations. These, however, have not violated the framework. Indeed it may be said that they have humanized the *British North America Act.* They have given it the elasticity of life. They have rescued it from the uncritical worship due to an imperishable and immutable relic of rigid antiquarianism. They, too, have contributed to political theory. In Canada are being worked out experiments in sovereignty. Or rather Canada is making a serious contribution to the destruction of the Austinian idea. Every province is from one point of view at least—in relation to the federal government—an example of a group with a life and purpose of its own. The history of education in the province of Manitoba is an interesting contribution to the decline and fall of the sovereign state.

In conclusion, there are two further distinctions between a federation and a confederation which have been made. They are not important, but need not be overlooked. Firstly, "a federal state is one all parts of which are represented, for international purposes, by one Government; and a confederation of states one whose governments retain the right to be separately

[1] Riddell, *op. cit.*, p. 98.

represented and considered."[1] Without discussing the definition it is obvious that, in so far as Canada is allowed international relations by the imperial tie, Canada is a federation. The Dominion government acts for Canada as a whole in any international affairs, including those of the Empire. Secondly, a federation is "a union of component states, wherein there is a central legislature which has authority to pass laws directly obligatory upon the people, the component states also having legislative power. In confederations, on the other hand, the central body has relations with the component states only, and not directly with individuals, *e.g.*, Austria-Hungary".[2] The inference in relation to Canada is obvious. From another aspect we may accept Judge Clement's opinion of the nature of Canadian government: "The true federal idea is clearly manifest, to recognize national unity with the right of local self-government; the very same idea that is stamped on the written Constitution of the United States."[3]

[1] Lewis, *On the Use and Abuse of some Political Terms* (ed. Raleigh, 1898), p. 97.
[2] Scott, *The Canadian Constitution Historically Explained* (1918), p. 3.
[3] Clement, *The Law of the Canadian Constitution*, p. 337.

CPSIA information can be obtained
at www.ICGtesting.com
Printed in the USA
LVHW080757190422
716542LV00001B/5